The United States in the New Asia

COUNCIL *on* FOREIGN RELATIONS

International Institutions and Global Governance Program

Council Special Report No. 50
November 2009

Evan A. Feigenbaum
Robert A. Manning

The United States in the New Asia

The Council on Foreign Relations (CFR) is an independent, nonpartisan membership organization, think tank, and publisher dedicated to being a resource for its members, government officials, business executives, journalists, educators and students, civic and religious leaders, and other interested citizens in order to help them better understand the world and the foreign policy choices facing the United States and other countries. Founded in 1921, CFR carries out its mission by maintaining a diverse membership, with special programs to promote interest and develop expertise in the next generation of foreign policy leaders; convening meetings at its headquarters in New York and in Washington, DC, and other cities where senior government officials, members of Congress, global leaders, and prominent thinkers come together with CFR members to discuss and debate major international issues; supporting a Studies Program that fosters independent research, enabling CFR scholars to produce articles, reports, and books and hold roundtables that analyze foreign policy issues and make concrete policy recommendations; publishing *Foreign Affairs*, the preeminent journal on international affairs and U.S. foreign policy; sponsoring Independent Task Forces that produce reports with both findings and policy prescriptions on the most important foreign policy topics; and providing up-to-date information and analysis about world events and American foreign policy on its website, www.cfr.org.

The Council on Foreign Relations takes no institutional position on policy issues and has no affiliation with the U.S. government. All statements of fact and expressions of opinion contained in its publications are the sole responsibility of the author or authors.

Council Special Reports (CSRs) are concise policy briefs, produced to provide a rapid response to a developing crisis or contribute to the public's understanding of current policy dilemmas. CSRs are written by individual authors—who may be CFR fellows or acknowledged experts from outside the institution—in consultation with an advisory committee, and are intended to take sixty days from inception to publication. The committee serves as a sounding board and provides feedback on a draft report. It usually meets twice—once before a draft is written and once again when there is a draft for review; however, advisory committee members, unlike Task Force members, are not asked to sign off on the report or to otherwise endorse it. Once published, CSRs are posted on www.cfr.org.

For further information about CFR or this Special Report, please write to the Council on Foreign Relations, 58 East 68th Street, New York, NY 10065, or call the Communications office at 212.434.9888. Visit our website, www.cfr.org.

Printed in the United States of America.

To submit a letter in response to a Council Special Report for publication on our website, www.cfr.org, you may send an email to CSReditor@cfr.org. Alternatively, letters may be mailed to us at: Publications Department, Council on Foreign Relations, 58 East 68th Street, New York, NY 10065. Letters should include the writer's name, postal address, and daytime phone number. Letters may be edited for length and clarity, and may be published online. Please do not send attachments. All letters become the property of the Council on Foreign Relations and will not be returned. We regret that, owing to the volume of correspondence, we cannot respond to every letter.

This report is printed on paper certified by the Forest Stewardship Council, which promotes environmentally responsible, socially beneficial, and economically viable management of the world's forests.

FSC
Mixed Sources
Product group from well-managed forests and other controlled sources
www.fsc.org Cert no. SW-COC-001530
© 1996 Forest Stewardship Council

Contents

Foreword

No region of the world today is more dynamic than Asia. Across the continent, booming countries have built engines of economic growth that have lifted hundreds of millions out of poverty. Along with this economic strength has come increased strategic importance, leading to Asia's emergence as a principal center of global power in the twenty-first century.

An essential question associated with Asia's rise is how to build a multilateral framework capable of effectively channeling the region's energies. Notwithstanding its economic and political advances, Asia faces a range of challenges. Critical issues, such as the division of the Korean Peninsula and the status of Taiwan, are unresolved. Lingering historical grievances persist between some of the region's major powers. And several countries face enormous internal hurdles, ranging from economic inequality to serious shortcomings in governance, that could produce scenarios capable of threatening regional stability. The task for policymakers—both in Asia and in other countries with interests in the region—is to develop multilateral institutions that can help manage these challenges while facilitating further economic and political gains.

In this Council Special Report, commissioned by CFR's International Institutions and Global Governance program, Evan A. Feigenbaum and Robert A. Manning examine Asia's regional architecture and consider what it means for the United States. They identify shortcomings in the region's existing multilateral mix and contend that this is not simply an Asian concern. Instead, the United States must increase its involvement in shaping Asian institutions in order to advance U.S. strategic interests and protect the competitiveness of American firms.

To do this, the authors outline six principles for U.S. policy toward Asia as a whole and recommend particular policies toward Northeast and Southeast Asia. Among other steps, they urge the United States to maintain a strong presence at Asian meetings; avoid intractable security issues and focus instead on topics ripe for cooperation; make use of ad hoc groupings as well as formal ones; and view some Asian institutions that exclude the United States as acceptable or even desirable, just as with the European Union.

The United States in the New Asia offers a rich analysis of Asia's multilateral landscape and makes a strong case for why it matters to the United States. The report also presents thoughtful recommendations for how Washington can influence this landscape in ways beneficial to American interests. The result is a document with important implications for U.S. policy toward a region that promises to play a central role in shaping the coming era of history.

Richard N. Haass
President
Council on Foreign Relations
November 2009

Acknowledgments

We are enormously grateful to the members of our advisory committee, whose names are listed at the back of this report. They offered trenchant critiques, historical perspective, a lesson or two in economics, and much support. CFR President Richard N. Haass read an early draft of our paper and encouraged us to publish it as a Council Special Report. James M. Lindsay, CFR's director of studies, gave us advice and assistance throughout.

Daniel Michaeli provided extraordinary research assistance and helpful critiques, and brought his wonderful enthusiasm to the project. We owe much to Patricia Dorff and Lia C. Norton in Publications, and to Lisa Shields, Leigh-Ann Krapf, and Sarah Doolin in Communications and Marketing.

This publication is part of CFR's International Institutions and Global Governance (IIGG) program and has been made possible by the generous support of the Robina Foundation. We are especially grateful to the IIGG's director, Stewart M. Patrick, an old colleague from our days on the State Department's policy planning staff. We could not be more delighted to be contributing to the IIGG's work.

Evan A. Feigenbaum
Robert A. Manning

Council Special Report

Introduction

President Barack Obama heads to Singapore in November for the 2009 Asia-Pacific Economic Cooperation forum (APEC) summit. It will be his first foray into the arcane world of Asian multilateralism. And if his administration adopts a new approach, it could yet fashion a more sustainable role for the United States in a changing Asia.

For more than a decade, creating multilateral forums has rivaled badminton as the leading indoor sport of Asian academics, think tanks, and governments. But the United States has mostly watched from the sidelines as proposals multiply and Asians organize themselves into an alphabet soup of new multilateral groups.

Most of these recent efforts have produced exceptionally modest results. Symbolism aside, would Asia be any less secure without the Association of Southeast Asian Nations (ASEAN) Regional Forum? What about the Thai-sponsored Asian Cooperation Dialogue, which includes Bahrain and Bhutan but not the United States, or the misnamed "East Asia Summit," which includes India from the subcontinent and New Zealand from Oceania? Would the security, economic, and environmental challenges of East Asia become any harder to address if these forums ceased to exist?

It is easy for Americans to dismiss such ventures as irrelevant in a region populated by big powers, where bilateral alliances and ancient strategic rivalries still loom large. That would be a mistake.

Yes, traditional balances of power endure in Asia. But there are at least three reasons why U.S. decision-makers ought to take Asian architecture seriously.

First, Asians themselves take architecture seriously and view multilateral institutions and agreements as essential to the development of their region. Washington's credibility in Asia, so important to a host of U.S. interests, depends, as it has since 1945, on whether and how the United States adapts to Asian interests, judgments, and goals.

Second, the United States might yet persuade Asians to fashion a more effective architecture in the future—one that will help secure its interests in the region.

Third, and not least, some multilateral institutions that exclude the United States have become the locus of economic and financial trends that will increasingly disadvantage U.S. firms and work against U.S. objectives. Certain preferential trade agreements and financial arrangements, as well as regionally based regulations and standards, threaten American interests. And some of the new institutions created without U.S. involvement, notably ASEAN Plus Three,* hold the potential to marginalize the United States in Asia over time.

For this reason, America's traditional "hub and spokes" approach to the region—with the United States as the hub, bilateral alliances as the spokes, and multilateral institutions largely at the margins of U.S. policy—is unsustainable. The United States will pay increasing costs to its interests, credibility, and influence unless it acts to shape multilateral trends in Asia.

China is becoming a locomotive for other Asian economies and lies at the center of the region's supply and production chains. But even at a time of global financial crisis, the United States continues to bring the greatest capacity to the table on the greatest number of issues vital to the future of the region. Surveys show that pluralities of strategic elites in Asia continue to view the United States as an essential strategic balancer, vital to stability.[1] And at least some of the boldest new proposals for future regional institutions, such as Australian prime minister Kevin Rudd's proposal of a new "Asia Pacific Community," incorporate the United States precisely because Washington retains enduring interests and offers unique capabilities vital to Asia's future.[2]

A *purposeful* multilateralism that pools the efforts of those with the greatest capacity could make Asia a more prosperous and secure region. By leading with new ideas and much more vigorous economic engagement by the administration, the United States can help define new roles for itself in a changing Asia.

*The ten ASEAN member states (Brunei, Cambodia, Indonesia, Laos, Malaysia, Myanmar, the Philippines, Singapore, Thailand, and Vietnam) plus China, Japan, and South Korea.

Form Over Function?

Achieving this more purposeful multilateralism will require leadership by and among Asia's big powers, as well as adjustments to how the United States and others have sought to construct multilateral institutions in Asia. If groups are to emerge that enable those with the greatest capacity to tackle specific problems, they will require a greater focus on function than form.

But unfortunately, form, not function, has been the principal driver of nearly all Asian multilateralism for more than a decade. Process has become an end in itself as Asians have formed redundant group after redundant group, often with the same membership, closely overlapping agendas, and precious little effect on regional or global problems. Senior officials meet regularly through these institutions, and that is a good thing. But none of them has taken collective action in the face of Asia's most recent urgent problems. In the tsunami of 2004, the East Timor crisis of 2006, the avian influenza epidemic of 2007, and the Myanmar cyclone of 2008, regional institutions were overshadowed by ad hoc international responses, frequently led by the United States.

One of the ironies of modern Asia is that Southeast Asians built most regional groups, even though the region's economic, military, and diplomatic power resides overwhelmingly in Northeast Asia. Together, China, Japan, South Korea, Russia, and the United States comprise close to 45 percent of global gross domestic product. They include the world's three largest economies and hold some 50 percent of global foreign exchange reserves. They are its largest consumers of energy, its largest emitters of greenhouse gases, and, with the possible exception of France and India, the world's leading proponents of civil nuclear power. They include major nuclear weapons states, three of five permanent members of the United Nations Security Council, and some of the world's principal sources of patents for technological innovation.

How did this mismatch come about? How did the part of East Asia with so much less economic, technological, and military capacity become the principal architect of nearly every recent effort to pool Asian power and capacity?

It is in part an accident of history. At the end of the Cold War, many Asians worried the United States, which had underpinned security in East Asia since 1945, would declare victory and simply go home. ASEAN—a collection of less powerful, Southeast Asian states—called for dialogues to keep the major players, including the United States, engaged in the region. The major powers, from Tokyo to Washington, had no qualms about participating in ASEAN-centric dialogues because such dialogues did not impinge on their interests.

In fact, creating such a balance in their relations with major powers was *precisely* what ASEAN states had in mind. For ASEAN, balancing the role of great powers to the north—China and Japan—had long provided an important impetus to regional community building. And concern about China, in particular, helped drive the transformation of ASEAN after the end of the Vietnam War.

ASEAN ultimately survived the end of a threat that had provided a source of its cohesion by bringing reunified Vietnam into the ASEAN fold. Put bluntly, ASEAN states believed they could more effectively balance China's growing weight and influence if Hanoi were safely inside the ASEAN tent. Thus, as China sought to "cherry-pick" the region—dealing with issues bilaterally, so its size and power might tilt the playing field in its favor—ASEAN countries sought to foster greater balance by discussing issues with China collectively. And in some areas, such as the South China Sea, China accommodated their concerns, bolstering ASEAN's faith in its strategy.

Asia Resurgent

But the proliferation of new multilateral groups in Asia must be viewed in another context as well. Since the end of the Cold War, the world has been in transition from an era defined by what it is not (the post–Cold War world) to a world in which a label has yet to stick. The driving force for an increasingly integrated world has been globalization, particularly in East Asia, where trans-Pacific trade and investment mushroomed after the Vietnam War, and where intra-Asian trade and investment took off even faster after 1991. Before the recent economic crisis, intra-Asian trade had surpassed even that within the North American Free Trade Agreement (NAFTA). Viewed in this light, the rise of new forums coincides with Asia's coming of age as the hub of the global economy.

Indeed, Asia's growing web of connections was especially reinforced by the 1997–98 financial crisis, which hit hardest in places like Indonesia and Thailand. Across the region, elites came to view the United States as arrogant and aloof, dictating clichéd solutions to skeptical Asians. And the United States, which had bailed out Mexico in 1994, refused to bail out Thailand just three years later, fueling perceptions that it neglected Southeast Asia. The United States continues to pay a price for those perceptions to this day.[3]

In this context, Asians groped for their own solutions. And, more than any other factor, the traumas of 1997 and 1998 became an inflection point, spurring the most recent wave of pan-Asian multilateralism.

Those years were the turning point—the moment that provided the impetus for Asia-only approaches that exclude the United States, and which also spurred Asia's turn away from APEC in favor of the ASEAN Plus Three, which has become the most coherent and substantive pan-Asian grouping. In that sense, the 1997–98 crisis comingled with a long-standing desire among some Asians to forge cohesion out of their region's enormous differences.

It is worth comparing Europe and Asia in this regard, since the comparison illuminates stark differences and illustrates many of the legacies Asians have sought to overcome.

Europeans have been linked since the end of the Roman Empire by a sense of the political and economic interrelationships among the various parts of their region, by Christianity as their dominant religion, and by their subsequent historical struggles with Islam. European collective identity found expression in the concept of the Holy Roman Empire, the Treaty of Westphalia, and the Concert of Vienna.

But a jumble of British, French, Dutch, Portuguese, Spanish, American, and other colonialisms marked Asia's modern history. And Asians not only experienced different colonial regimes, but were divided by Buddhist, Confucian, Muslim, Hindu, and Christian religious traditions as well.

Contemporary Asian regionalism—and the desire to forge at least some pan-Asian cohesion out of these enormous differences—has found expression across Asia. Take postwar Japan, a U.S. ally with a strong sense of trans-Pacific identity. Even as it has nurtured a robust alliance with the United States, Japan and its bureaucracy have incubated a variety of Asian regional ideas and ideologies, especially with respect to Asian monetary integration.[4] It was Japanese officials who in 1997 proposed the establishment of an Asian Monetary Fund, a proposal that helped give rise to today's Chiang Mai Initiative of bilateral swaps among the ASEAN Plus Three countries.[5] And a new Japanese government under Yukio Hatoyama—the first non–Liberal Democratic Party government in nearly two decades—now envisions an East Asian Community, although its details are vague and probably fragmentary even in Tokyo.[6]

The responses that emerged from the 1997–98 crisis—Asia-only bond funds, Asia-only currency swaps such as Chiang Mai, and Asia-only trade and investment pacts—built on existing concepts and frameworks. They built, too, on the region's principal existing multilateral entity, ASEAN. Today's ASEAN Plus Three, the East Asia Summit, and functional ideas such as Chiang Mai have their origin in (or were lent new impetus by) this searing experience of 1997–98.

But pan-Asian solutions have had little utility in the midst of the first truly global financial crisis. And, with the exception of the Six Party Talks on North Korea's nuclear program, most of the new formations in the region are centered on process, not function or measurable results, and are unwieldy, with too many actors who lack capacity and thus bring too little to the table on too many issues.

Contrast, for instance, what Japan and China can do to fight financial contagion with what Laos and Myanmar, or even Vietnam, can realistically do. Sadly, the same is true of some of the region's leading trans-Pacific institutions: Is Asia better positioned to fight today's financial crisis because APEC has twenty-one member economies instead of just the nine that are also in the Group of Twenty (G20)? Or is APEC stronger for including Papua New Guinea and Peru while excluding India, an Asian giant soon to be a top five global economy that is increasingly connected to East Asia?

With or without the participation of the United States, regional groups in Asia duplicate one another's roles. They have too many members, and mostly lack functionality or a comprehensive template to measure and systematically assess results. They have developed habits of dialogue, but social interchange and political rhetoric dominate. Lingering suspicions and historical anxieties remain. Asian concerns about maintaining "face" have typically meant that the most sensitive topics, from human rights to territorial disputes, are avoided. The ASEAN Regional Forum is perhaps the best example of this. It is Asia's leading security forum, and yet all of the potential sources of major conflict—China-Taiwan, Korea, India-Pakistan, and sensitive territorial disputes—are off the table.

For groups to emerge that can solve real problems by pooling real capabilities, function will need to drive form, not the other way around. And function ultimately will need to be married to capacity, with those that have the greatest capacity playing the most significant roles. For the United States to lead, albeit as an increasingly equal partner, Washington must demonstrate to Asians that a redefined U.S. role will be important if a coherent and purposeful architecture for twenty-first century Asia is to emerge from the present stew.

Wake Up, America

The reality to which the United States must adapt is that Asians are redefining their region, trying to develop a sense of "Asian" identity and enhance their clout in the global system. Some forums, including pan-Asian groups that exclude the United States, are inevitable because meetings, seminars, summits, and ministerials are so deeply embroidered into the fabric of East Asian international relations. But these groups now include a nascent pan-Asian trade and financial architecture, with regionalism becoming one layer of the emerging multilayered international system. One challenge, then, is to ensure that Asia's regionalism is consistent with global norms and practices, including, for instance, those of the World Trade Organization (WTO).

The good news is that Americans have woken up—although a failure by the Obama administration to reinvigorate trade policy, or a resurgent protectionism, could dramatically undermine America's position in Asia. At least a serious debate about architecture is finally under way in the United States, building in part on the experience of the Six Party Talks, one of the few groups formed with a well-defined and specific functional agenda. Washington has at last acceded to the ASEAN Treaty of Amity and Cooperation as its Asian partners urged for years.[7] And on a bipartisan basis, Americans advocate greater Asian involvement in the G20 and a role for Asia in the international financial institutions commensurate with its economic and financial weight.

Indeed, one outcome of the September 2009 Pittsburgh G20 is that decisions were taken that supplant the Group of Eight (G8), with the G20 becoming the new high table for managing the global economy. The G20 may thus become an important venue and interface for the United States with Asia, especially after G20 members decided in Pittsburgh to increase the shares of developing countries in the International Monetary Fund (IMF) and World Bank by 5 percent and 3 percent, respectively. A prospective Asia-Pacific "caucus" in the G20 might offer such a mechanism, allowing the United States to forge trans-Pacific approaches to regional and global issues with China, Japan, India, South Korea, Indonesia, and Australia within the G20 context.

All of this is welcome, and part of a gradual but unmistakable reshaping of the global order of which Asia is an increasingly central component. But make no mistake: a more serious American attitude toward Asian architecture reflects a change of approach, and a bipartisan one at that.

For more than a decade, through two administrations, both Democratic and Republican, the United States responded to Asian entreaties that it get serious about multilateralism by chanting "we like APEC" in response to nearly every Asian proposal for a new group. But APEC, too, meets none of the crucial tests: it is large, unwieldy, and built around an ill-defined "Pacific community" that almost inexplicably includes small Latin American economies, some of whose principal connection to Asia is having a beach on the Pacific Ocean. Indeed, APEC, like many of the new pan-Asian groups, mismatches countries of widely varying sizes, endowments, and capabilities.

As a Pacific, but not "Asian," power, the United States needs to base its efforts on a hardheaded assessment of what tables it needs to sit at and when and where it can afford to step aside. The United States was once the preeminent power in Asia and in most respects remains the critical extraregional actor and strategic balancer. But primacy no longer means hegemony. One way to think about current trends is to recognize that the post–World War II primacy the United States enjoyed in Asia was a historical anomaly. The reemergence of Japan, China, India, and Asia writ large returns Asia to the global stature it enjoyed in the preindustrial period.

Adapting American primacy to the realities of the new Asia means accepting that some pan-Asian forums are here to stay and will become central to the region's political landscape. Americans must understand that, just as the United States is not a member of the European Union, Washington does not need to sit in every room or join every conversation to pursue its core interests in Asia. The policy challenge is to integrate some pan-Asian and trans-Pacific groupings while ensuring that others function in complementary ways.

Déjà Vu

The bad news is that the most widely discussed ideas for reinvigorating U.S. leadership replicate the very weaknesses of existing frameworks. Americans and Asians increasingly share a tendency to promote overlapping arrangements of groups, including groups of vague purpose, as, in themselves, a solution to Asia's problems.

Take one idea: the proposed U.S.-China-Japan trilateral process, which Secretary of State Hillary Rodham Clinton endorsed in a February 19, 2009, interview with Japan's *Asahi Shimbun*, now temporarily stalled but likely to begin eventually with trilateral policy planning talks.[8]

The new group cuts out the other principal U.S. ally in Northeast Asia, South Korea. It risks irrelevance if it ducks the hard issues, such as competing Chinese and Japanese territorial claims, Japanese concerns about China's military posture, and Chinese suspicions about the U.S.-Japan alliance and missile defense. And it will create frustration or even increased tension if it does try to delve into such tough issues. Although the new group will grope for purpose, it is not obvious what issues or capabilities are unique to these three actors and do not already exist in other multilateral forums.

What is more, the new U.S.-China-Japan trilateral joins a confusing welter of at least five existing Asian trilaterals: U.S.-Japan-South Korea, China-Japan-South Korea, U.S.-Japan-Australia, China-India-Russia, and U.S.-Japan-India. The latter three countries conduct the Malabar military exercise, but some in New Delhi, Tokyo, and Washington advocate expanding their cooperation through coordinated diplomatic and strategic efforts. And among some in the four capitals, lingering sentiment remains for a prospective quadrilateral bringing the United States, Japan, Australia, and India together.

Is there a purpose to all this redundant and overlapping geometry? What is unique to any of these groups of three or four that would enable enduring solutions to the most pressing security, economic, or transnational problems? There are almost no issues of significance that any of these existing or proposed trilateral or quadrilateral groups can resolve working alone.

Start with energy security, which some have suggested is the most promising agenda item for a U.S.-China-Japan group, including the *Asahi*'s respected editor in chief, Yoichi Funabashi.[9]

Why not include Russia, potentially the major new source of regional oil and gas supply? There is already an Asia-Pacific Partnership on Clean Development and Climate that includes the United States, China, Japan, South Korea, India, and Australia, as well as a China-initiated energy ministers' dialogue among five of these six countries, excluding only Australia. There is a raft of existing multinational technology-based initiatives that include most of these countries. And there is the Major Economies Meeting on Energy Security and Climate Change that includes seventeen of the most important economies.

How about financial coordination, another prospective subject for the U.S.-China-Japan (and China-Japan-South Korea) trilateral? Why would the United States, China, and Japan not include Europe in a G4, given that the euro is an international reserve currency, albeit on a smaller scale than the dollar, and the four largely dominate global finance? Or why not coordinate instead among central bankers of the world's largest reserve currency, the United States, and the largest holders of dollar foreign exchange reserves, such as China, Japan, Singapore, and South Korea?

Back to First Principles

A more effective and purposeful multilateralism would begin with lessons learned. Neither Asia nor the world lacks a history of successful multinational coordination. But especially since the end of the Cold War, the most successful multilateral groups have been ad hoc and informal, mobilizing specific coalitions to address specific issues, imminent problems, and immediate crises.

Crisis has tended to be the catalyst of such successful multilateral ventures. But Asia's redundant existing mishmash reflects an underlying assumption that dialogue and process are beneficial in and of themselves. Thus geometries have been created only to grope for missions and functions.

At some level, this reflects the liberal institutionalist view that well-functioning institutions in themselves can mediate problems and ambitions. But recent experience, certainly in Asia, suggests that institutions are only as useful as the major powers are invested in them. The prevailing approach has devalued most of Asia's existing architectures while doing little to foster a more effective one: in every crisis of recent years, the most effective global and regional problem-solving has been borne of necessity and focused on results.

The most successful groups have assembled quick-moving countries, animated by the urgency of crises, that combine interest, resources, and expertise. They eschew the big international security questions that so preoccupy think tanks and academe. They are unencumbered by ritualistic institutions and attendant bureaucracies. And they focus on discrete, often imminent problems.

Consider the Tsunami Core Group, through which the United States, Japan, Australia, and India provided rapid and effective relief around the Indian Ocean for nine days in 2004 and 2005. As former undersecretary of state Marc Grossman has put it, the Core Group "was an organization that never met in one of diplomacy's storied cities, never issued a communiqué, never created a secretariat, and took as one of its successes its own demise." Indeed, the group was effective precisely because it was ad hoc—its members "could spend serious money to deploy capable and sustainable forces to deal with crises."[10]

The same goes for the ad hoc response to avian influenza, which demonstrates that the United States is hardly the only power in the Pacific attracted to ad hoc multilateralism. China played an important convening role in organizing a 2006 pledging conference and promoted international coordination after an initial U.S. call to action. Or take the 2008 Myanmar cyclone, when India, Thailand, Malaysia, and others joined the United States in quickly organizing ad hoc relief mechanisms.

The lesson is straightforward: first identify the functional problem, and then assemble the right group of players. Put differently: avoid geometry for its own sake. Form should follow function, and any multilateral group in Asia is more likely to be effective if it assembles those with the greatest power and capacity and has a clear, agreed purpose. Heads of state, ministers, and senior officials can and must meet on some regular basis, both regionally and globally. For this reason, having an overarching forum where leaders come together on a regular basis can be a useful foundation from which to assemble effective mechanisms, whether ad hoc or more enduring. But durable and effective groupings are more likely to emerge from demonstrated common purpose than from abstract geometry.[11]

It is not, to be sure, difficult to understand why and how so many Asian institutions took form, not function, as their touchstone. ASEAN, whose members have historically lacked mutual trust for many reasons, is the best example. In the case of ASEAN, putting form first was not an alternative to putting some useful function first, but an alternative to the member states' continued near isolation. Form helped ASEAN countries, or at least the original six, become comfortable with one another and familiar with nearby leaders.

But more than forty years have passed since ASEAN took shape. And whether in ASEAN or in Asia writ large, disparities of capacity and conflicting objectives make it difficult to address functional challenges in large groups or most established institutions.

At a moment of historic transition there is good cause to reevaluate existing institutions and modify them as necessary to adjust to current realities. At the global level, recent discussion of change in the management of the IMF is one positive example of this. There ought to be a sense of experimentation in efforts to fashion new forums. But innovation has been sadly lacking in both pan-Asian and Asia-Pacific groupings. Instead, the region has seen a good deal of hollow process, driven by bureaucratic inertia or path dependence: groups are formed, ritualistically meet, ritualistically issue statements, and then ritualistically persist.

Rules to Live By

Six rules of thumb could guide a more effective U.S. approach. They can be applied consistently, both to big formal groups, such as APEC, and to smaller ad hoc groups.

1. *Show up.* Until a new, more functional approach emerges, the United States pays a price when the president or cabinet secretaries cancel trips and skip regional gatherings. These gatherings achieve little—and that is precisely why it is time for a new, more functional approach to Asian architecture. But there are huge symbolic political costs to U.S. absence from existing gatherings. Every skipped meeting reinforces doubts about U.S. credibility, undermining Washington's ability to promote a different approach.

2. *Avoid core security issues and focus instead on what is practical.* Why? Efforts to fashion a new security architecture for East Asia have gone nowhere for several reasons: America's Asian alliances dissuade security competition, provide reassurance, and remain the backbone of East Asian security; there is simply no basis for collective security among China, Japan, and South Korea; and collective security is inconceivable prior to Korean reunification and a mutually satisfactory resolution of Taiwan's status.

This means the United States will want to continually reinforce and adapt its alliances. And it will want to resist any effort to use regional arrangements that exclude Washington to undermine those vital relationships. North Korea's nuclear and missile tests only reinforce to many in the region the value of the existing—and long-standing—U.S. security guarantee. And in the coming decade and perhaps beyond, that desire for the U.S. security guarantee in Asia is unlikely to diminish. In the interim, nearly every power in Asia is hedging against uncertainty: What are China's intentions? What are Japan's goals?

Until the central questions of Korea and Taiwan are resolved, not to mention a welter of knotty bilateral and multilateral territorial disputes—and until China and Japan come to terms with each other in a manner similar to that of the Franco-German reconciliation—there is no basis for cooperative or collective security in the Pacific. Calls for an Asian equivalent of the Organization for Security and Cooperation in Europe and the like have fallen on deaf ears for this very reason.[12]

3. *Do not limit U.S. thinking to the formal groups.* Habits of cooperation emerge from mutual interests, shared objectives, and, as with the Tsunami Core Group, joint efforts to confront real problems. The success of ad hoc responses in recent years suggests a premium on informality and flexibility.

4. *Acknowledge that even as Asian powers assume global responsibilities, they will remain attracted to many aspects of regionalism.* The global system is multilayered, complex, and fluid. When the dust clears from the current financial crisis, the character of economic globalization may be significantly changed with respect to capital flows, production chains, and trade patterns in Asia.

In East Asia, it is ASEAN Plus Three that will, most likely, be at the core of this new regionalism. The group is likely to focus on an economic agenda that challenges traditional American approaches and certainly disadvantages U.S. firms.

If Japanese and Korean firms enjoy tariff-free treatment of the manufactures they sell in China while U.S. firms face the current average most-favored nation rate of 9 percent, American firms will lose substantial sales in an import market worth well over one trillion dollars. And they will lose substantial sales in Korea and Japan, too, as ASEAN Plus Three moves toward further tariff reduction.

ASEAN Plus Three is on a trajectory to become the locus of intra-Asian trade liberalization. And, with Asians unlikely to embrace the United States as a member of ASEAN Plus Three, the United States needs not just to take intra-Asian trade liberalization efforts more seriously, but to conclude the Doha round so that multilateral liberalization can erase such intraregional trade preferences. Otherwise, U.S. economic losses will mount.

ASEAN Plus Three may also become the locus of intensified discussion of Asian monetary interests. Thus, the United States ought to prepare for the Chinese renminbi, in the words of World Bank president

Robert B. Zoellick, to "evolve into a force in financial markets"—even if that remains a generation away.[13]

5. *Do not balk at every pan-Asian institution that excludes the United States.* Washington can hardly tell the world's leading economies that they are not allowed to speak to one another without Americans in every room and in every conversation. Neither can the United States have NAFTA or a Free Trade Area of the Americas while telling Asians they cannot pursue pan-Asian trade arrangements. Some pan-Asian formations are inevitable, and the United States should view them similarly to its support for European institutions.

The fact is, most pan-Asian institutions will move forward regardless of American views and preferences. So the Asian groups that merit vigilance from Washington are those that pursue functional agendas detrimental to American economic or security interests, such as preferential trade agreements.

But the United States will need to carefully calibrate its responses. Some of the closest U.S. allies in Asia are actively promoting pan-Asian arrangements that exclude the United States—for instance, Japan and South Korea through ASEAN Plus Three, and Japanese prime minister Hatoyama through his East Asian Community. For the moment, then, an immediate challenge to the United States is that its allies are, in some cases, facilitating meaningful pan-Asian architectures that exclude it. Washington's first response should be to consult closely with Canberra, Seoul, and Tokyo to encourage coordination and, where possible, joint efforts.

But that is not enough, and so a sixth and final rule will be essential:

6. *Start leading, not least by presenting the region in a consultative manner with new ideas, including for ad hoc multilateral cooperation.* The United States, quite simply, can no longer succeed without adapting to these realities of a new Asia. This means it will need to offer a credible alternative vision, not least by strengthening its own trans-Pacific and global trade engagement but also by suggesting innovative ways to streamline regional institutions. Americans and Asians need to think together about how and where trans-Pacific and pan-Asian institutions should intersect and reinforce each other.

This would usefully begin with a serious conversation with allies and partners about what the experiments in Asian multilateralism have wrought in the two decades since the end of the Cold War.

Asian governments themselves complain about redundant institutions with overlapping agendas and a deficit of results. Privately, many concede a growing need to streamline and rationalize Asian architecture.

So why not join with those Asian voices? For instance, Hadi Soesastro, a leading Indonesian economist, argues that "what needs to be attempted is to reform and restructure the existing mechanisms so that they become key elements of a more coherent and consolidated regional process."[14] Indonesia's leading strategist, Jusuf Wanandi, has proposed merging the two mostly redundant leaders' summits—APEC and the East Asia Summit—one of which includes the United States, the other of which does not.

Wanandi calls for "a regional institution that could accommodate the three big powers—China, India, and Japan—in a kind of concert of power that will be able to maintain future equilibrium in the region, together with the United States." Thus, he concludes, "regional architecture in East Asia and the Asia-Pacific needs consolidation."[15]

Merging the two leaders' summits would link pan-Asian with trans-Pacific institutions in just this way, and it would continue to provide an overarching forum from which to assemble both ad hoc and enduring functional mechanisms. Indeed, much as the ASEAN Regional Forum functions as Asia's security ministerial, the region could convert APEC from a summit into its economic ministerial, fully melded into a new, more integrated architecture. Or else, leaders' meetings could simply be rotated between APEC and an expanded East Asia Summit. Either way, the result would be cleaner and much more efficient: one summit, two functionally specific ministerials, loosely connected. And Taiwan, which attends APEC but no other regional group because of Chinese objections, would not suffer drastically because its unofficial representation would be unaffected by whether APEC is held as a summit or as a ministerial.

The time is ripe for this sort of fresh thinking because even those who have been most closely associated with the APEC process now raise first-order questions about whether it has a future. C. Fred Bergsten chaired APEC's Eminent Persons Group from 1993 to 1995. He puts the point succinctly: "Do the Asian members of APEC want a primarily Pacific Asia future (whether it is constructed via a 10+3, 10+6, or something else) or do they want an Asia Pacific dimension as well?" In a recent options paper, Bergsten (who would prefer that Asians join the

United States in rescuing and reinvigorating APEC) even offers "terminate APEC" as one of his options—for instance, if Asians should instead decide that their seats in the G20, combined with their sheer economic and political weight, are enough to protect Asian interests and ensure "respectful attention by the United States."[16] Bergsten's American voice has been joined by Asian voices. Barry Desker, a leading Singaporean strategist, is equally blunt: "If APEC fails to break new ground, it will soon fade."[17]

There have been potentially important, if modest, efforts among APEC members to move beyond consensus decision-making and take concrete steps toward WTO-compatible free trade expansion among those prepared to move forward. A P4 (New Zealand, Singapore, and Chile, later joined by Brunei) launched such an agreement in 2005, turning it into a P7 with Australia, Peru, and Vietnam in 2008. The United States joined the fray at the end of the Bush administration, dubbing it the Trans-Pacific Partnership (TPP). But even as Canada is now considering joining the agreement, the Obama administration has put U.S. participation on hold. Such steps could be the building blocks for an eventual Free Trade Area of the Asia-Pacific (FTAAP), but that remains a distant aspiration.

For Americans who believe a sustainable U.S. role in Asian architecture requires robust functional linkages, it is clearly time for the United States to lead creatively with friends and allies—perhaps by returning APEC to its economic roots, perhaps even by moving beyond APEC, but certainly through reinvigorated trade policies in the region.

Northeast Asia: Getting Serious

In the end, the greatest challenge to multilateral cooperation will lie in Northeast Asia. Collective security is inconceivable at present, but enduring solutions to a host of transnational issues will require cooperation among those with the maximum capacity and interest to solve them.

China, Japan, and South Korea (the Plus Three) have created a trilateral mechanism, focused mainly on economic issues. But addressing issues at the core of the Plus Three agenda—trade, investment, standards, and energy security—would be more effective and efficient if it included the capabilities of the United States. And the United States has tangible and vital interests in nearly everything that happens in Northeast Asia.

A good place to start pooling the resources of those with maximum capacity would be to expand this Plus Three to the five players who have cooperated in the Six Party process. Expansion from three to five would bring together the five major actors in the north Pacific who combine interest, resources, capacity, and expertise on a host of economic, environmental, transnational, and diplomatic questions. Converting the existing Plus Three into a forum that assembles the right players also offers a better chance than the proposed U.S.-China-Japan trilateral of ensuring lasting cooperation on a modest—but concrete—agenda for Northeast Asia.

This could be done in several ways. It could mean adding the United States and Russia to the existing Plus Three to create a formal five-party mechanism for Northeast Asia. It could also mean starting with five-party coordination on the margins of the G20.

A five-party mechanism is appealing on several levels: although the United States will have to stand aside as some pan-Asian institutions advance, it is, by virtue of geography and history, a Pacific power and especially a north Pacific power. Only twelve miles in the Bering Strait separate the United States from the Asian mainland. The United States has vital interests that suggest it will remain a north Pacific power for as far as the eye can see. Meaningful and effective Northeast Asian institutions ought to reflect that, both in their membership and agenda.

At the same time, the Six Party diplomacy has been a pathbreaking exercise. The North Koreans have stymied the ultimate objective of denuclearization, but the lesson for the other five is that they can still work well together when they share an overlapping interest and a focused, functional objective. They can work well together in a variety of ways, even if the sixth party ultimately prevented their earlier efforts from succeeding.

At various junctures, other countries sought to join the North Korea denuclearization dialogue. But these five—and no others—are at the table because each possesses a specific and material set of tools and core interests for addressing the nuclear problem. Each brought real capacity to the table—diplomatic, economic, or political. In this instance, as in few others in the history of Asian institution-building, form followed function and capacity determined who ultimately sat at the table.

In May 2004, the United States, recognizing the unique concentration of global power among these five countries, sought to explore this sort of five-party mechanism. It proposed five-party policy planning talks with a modest, but focused, agenda distinct from the question of North Korean denuclearization: oil and gas pipeline strategies, coordination of strategic petroleum reserves, localized environmental problems such as Asian "yellow dust" and "brown cloud," civil nuclear safety, public health policies, and regional economic cooperation.

The idea foundered—even though Japan and South Korea embraced it, and Russia offered a provisional yes—because China worried about North Korea's reaction and a resulting drag on the Six Party Talks.

But five years later, North Korea appears to be seeking deliverable nuclear weapons. It has tested two nuclear devices, launched two rockets, threatened further nuclear and missile tests, and generally isolated itself in the bargain. Pyongyang's rhetoric suggests it seeks to be dealt with in any future talks as a nuclear weapons state.

So whether North Korea eventually returns to the Six Party process—as it well may, as a result of Chinese blandishments—the other five countries have common interests quite apart from North Korea. And now more than ever, there is no reason to give Pyongyang a veto over the future of Northeast Asian cooperation, especially on issues where North Korea has few interests and brings zero capacity to the table.

On a rich agenda of transnational and economic issues, such as those that animated the 2004 U.S. proposal, the five have overlapping interests but pursue too few complementary policies. The three main powers of the region are also moving forward without the United States through their creation of the Plus Three, an outgrowth of the ASEAN Plus Three. In that setting, Beijing, Seoul, and Tokyo have sought breakthroughs not on the security questions that so preoccupy Americans but on bread-and-butter issues such as investment, trade, financial and exchange rate questions, regulatory standards, energy, and tourism.

That offers a more robust agenda for cooperation than the peace and security mechanism that has long been the focus of discussion in Northeast Asia. The Six Party Talks convened a constituent working group, including Pyongyang, to explore it. But the prospects for such a security mechanism are dim. If a breakthrough *were* achieved on North Korea, including, ultimately, a path to normalization of its relations with the United States and Japan, there would indeed be a rich, security-centered agenda for a six-party Northeast Asia forum. But such progress seems more distant than ever.

At this point, then, the more compelling rationale for security-related cooperation among the five is contingency planning, including managing the transition to an eventually reunified Korea. Given the political trajectory of North Korea as it falls further and further behind the rest of a dynamic Northeast Asia, managing change on the Korean Peninsula could offer an organizing principle. The five main players would be prudent to begin quietly discussing how to cope with various possible contingencies and responses—although this is something even South Korea and Japan, both allies of the United States, have historically found difficult to do. The five could pursue nontraditional security issues, such as disaster relief. But introducing China into the equation could make cooperation more difficult still. After China's 2008 Sichuan earthquake, for example, Chinese sensitivities precluded Tokyo from sending a C-130 carrying tents and blankets for the victims, so Japan had to opt instead for a charter.[18] Beijing has also been reluctant to discuss planning for humanitarian crises that could occur on the Korean Peninsula. Until the fundamental security dynamics in Northeast Asia change, the obstacles to any agenda that pursues regionwide cooperative or collective security remain high.

But there are more useful organizing principles than security cooperation, in any case. Expanding the Plus Three to five would bring additional capacity and resources to the table on a host of vital economic and transnational issues that have little to do with North Korea. The door could remain open to North Korea, largely symbolically. Beijing and Seoul would likely seek to include Pyongyang if its behavior were to change. And if North Korea's behavior were to improve dramatically, the greater security interests of the United States would argue for Pyongyang's inclusion as well. The fact remains, however, that the five have a qualitatively different role and status, and, unlike North Korea, they bring substance and tangible capabilities to the table on a rich menu of interests unrelated to security.

That reflects their economic, technological, strategic, environmental, and financial weight. Each brings something to the table that could contribute to a modest, clearly defined, results-oriented effort. And there is precedent on which to build: both the 2004 U.S. proposal for five-party policy planning talks and a subsequent Japanese proposal for a five-party Northeast Asia energy mechanism.

And Southeast Asia?

Meanwhile, the United States will need to continue and expand its robust engagement with Southeast Asia, not least because ASEAN will remain at the core of Asia's large, formal multilateral institutions. The ASEAN Regional Forum, ASEAN Plus Three, and other mechanisms are here to stay. And a U.S. presence is not only welcomed but expected in the forums and institutions in which Washington participates. But Washington is also well positioned to capitalize on enormous bilateral opportunities, especially with Indonesia and Vietnam. The United States has many more reasons to engage Southeast Asia than the future of regional institutions. And this suggests that Washington should not rely on ASEAN as its sole vehicle for such engagement.

Of course, even as the United States pursues ad hoc mechanisms and moves beyond ASEAN-centric multilateralism, it would be foolish to pay ASEAN no heed. Forty years of commitment to ASEAN has, in many ways, altered the fundamental dynamics between Southeast Asian states. The formation of ASEAN, which has grown to represent some 500 million people, was made possible by Indonesian president Suharto's abandonment of Sukarno's policy of *Konfrontasi* with Malaysia. But ASEAN gained its cohesion from shared concerns about communist expansion beyond Indochina, and it has successfully leveraged meetings at all levels of leadership and bureaucracy to foster a sense of common interest, reinforced by personal acquaintance with counterparts in other ASEAN capitals. It has also had some notable successes. ASEAN played a useful role, for example, in the 1991 Cambodian peace settlement. In a region once wracked by conflict, it is significant that war has never broken out between ASEAN members.

Quite appropriately, then, in September 2008 the United States became the first ASEAN dialogue partner to appoint an ambassador to ASEAN, an initiative spearheaded by Senator Richard G. Lugar (R-IN) and completed in the last months of the Bush administration.[19]

The United States now works with ASEAN through the ASEAN-U.S. Cooperation Plan announced in 2002; the ASEAN-U.S. Technical Assistance and Training Facility established inside the ASEAN secretariat in 2004; the ASEAN-U.S. Enhanced Partnership agreement signed in 2005; the Enhanced Partnership Plan of Action signed in 2006; the ASEAN-U.S. Trade and Investment Framework Agreement also established in 2006; and under the rubric of the Treaty of Amity and Cooperation, which the United States joined after the Obama administration took office in 2009.[20]

But although the United States has done well to reinforce its relationship with ASEAN, and thus its relationships in Southeast Asia, an intellectually honest appraisal should also acknowledge ASEAN's severe limitations. As Indonesia's Wanandi has bluntly put it, "ASEAN's limited cohesion has become a limiting factor.... [It is] increasingly doubtful whether ASEAN will be able to take the lead in institution-building."

Expansion of its membership to Indochina and Myanmar and the weakness of ASEAN's alphabetically rotating chairmanship have created structural limitations to ASEAN effectiveness. ASEAN's founding members, understandably, wanted all ten Southeast Asian countries joined as a cohesive force to help balance China. But their timing was poor: Myanmar could not be assimilated to ASEAN ways and—unlike Vietnam—Cambodia and Laos carry little weight. A "wise persons" commission asked to advise on the creation of an ASEAN charter recommended replacing consensus with majority decision-making, but the adopted charter has fallen short of this goal.

One question, then, is whether ASEAN members share the creativity the European Union has demonstrated in negotiating and attempting to ratify the Lisbon Treaty. Asia is not Europe, and Asian institutions can hardly be compared to the EU. But the Lisbon process, like the EU constitutional process that preceded it, has reflected a sense of trial and error and an effort to improve Europe's institutions. That process of experimentation continues apace in Europe.

ASEAN may change slowly, but Southeast Asia is changing dramatically. Thailand and the Philippines have become less coherent polities, less effective both inside and outside the ASEAN context. Indonesia, Singapore, and Vietnam have become more prominent and economically dynamic, with robust bilateral ties to the United States. As a vibrant new democracy and a member of the G20, Indonesia warrants special attention, not least because the Yudhoyono government seeks a broad-based partnership with the United States. Meanwhile, U.S.-Malaysia relations have improved on the basis of trade, counterterrorism cooperation, and military exchanges.

The United States has been doing more with ASEAN, especially through the Enhanced Partnership announced by the Bush administration in 2005. But it has also been doing more—much more—bilaterally. And given the considerable gap in military, economic, and diplomatic power between Northeast and Southeast Asia, there will always be serious limitations to ASEAN-centric multilateralism.

Conclusion

For so many reasons, the nature of American engagement in Asia will shape the region's future. But it is essential to adapt U.S. policy to the contours of change in Asia if the United States wishes to remain vital and relevant there. A generation hence, in 2030, the United States could find its firms at a competitive disadvantage in a part of the world that will constitute about half of the global economy. Already we see, for example, South Korea moving ahead on a free trade agreement with the European Union as the Korea-U.S. Free Trade Agreement languishes in Washington. And that is not the end of the story. The United States could find an Asia much less willing to accommodate its interests, and particularly its commercial, economic, and financial interests. Without vigorous engagement, especially multilateral trade engagement and liberalization, American credibility and influence will wane. Others will fill the vacuum.

The punch line, then, is this: President Obama has a unique opportunity to adapt U.S. policy to the new realities of a changing Asia. The starting point remains America's bilateral alliances and partnerships, which lie at the core of U.S. engagement with the region. But it is time to build on these rich, multifaceted relationships by exercising greater multilateral leadership in Asia and reinvigorating U.S. leadership on global and regional trade liberalization. And it is essential that the United States begin a serious conversation with its Asian partners about a more purposeful and functional multilateralism that respects Asia's trajectory while redefining how and where the United States fits into a twenty-first century Asia.

Endnotes

1. Bates Gill, Michael Green, Kiyoto Tsuji, and William Watts, *Strategic Views on Asian Regionalism: Survey Results and Analysis* (Washington, DC: Center for Strategic and International Studies, February 2009), p. 6.
2. Kevin Rudd, "It's Time to Build an Asia Pacific Community," address to the Asia Society AustralAsia Centre, Sydney, June 4, 2008, http://www.pm.gov.au/node/5763.
3. Morton Abramowitz and Stephen Bosworth, *Chasing the Sun: Rethinking East Asian Policy* (New York: Century Foundation Press, 2006), chapter 2; Ellen L. Frost, *Asia's New Regionalism* (Boulder, CO: Lynne Rienner, 2008), chapter 6.
4. Paul Volcker and Toyoo Gyoten, *Change of Fortune* (New York: New York Times Books, 1992); Toyoo Gyoten, "Steadily Towards the 'Asian Common Currency,'" *Nihon Keizai Shimbun*, March 13, 2003; Eisuke Sakakibara, "The Asian Monetary Fund: Where Do We Go From Here?" Institute of Strategic and International Studies International Conference on Globalization, February 26, 2001, http://www.map.gsec.keio.ac.jp/files/kl_feb01.pdf; Keiko Ujikane and Tatsuo Ito, "Asia Needs Own Monetary Fund to Stem Crisis, ADB's Kawai Says," *Bloomberg*, February 25, 2009, http://www.bloomberg.com/apps/news?pid=20601080&refer=asia&sid=acuxFHCbE5Vc; Hitoshi Tanaka, "A New Leadership Role for Japan," *Global Asia* 4, no. 1 (spring 2009), p. 15; Henrik Schmiegelow, "How 'Asian' Will Asia Be in the 21st Century?" *ASIEN 100* (July 2006), pp. 55–60, http://www.asienkunde.de/content/zeitschrift_asien/archiv/pdf/A100_054_061.pdf.
5. Phillip Y. Lipscy, "Japan's Asian Monetary Fund Proposal," *Stanford Journal of East Asian Affairs* 3 (summer 2003), pp. 93–104.
6. Yukio Hatoyama, "Address at the Sixty-Fourth Session of the General Assembly of the United Nations," September 24, 2009, http://www.mofa.go.jp/policy/UN/assembly2009/pm0924-2.html; "Japan, China to Work Together on Creating 'East Asia Community,'" *Japan Times*, September 29, 2009, http://search.japantimes.co.jp/cgi-bin/nn20090929a3.html.
7. U.S. Department of State, "United States Accedes to the Treaty of Amity and Cooperation in Southeast Asia," July 22, 2009, http://www.state.gov/r/pa/prs/ps/2009/july/126294.htm.
8. Hillary Rodham Clinton, interview by Yoichi Funabashi and Yoichi Kato, February 19, 2009, http://www.america.gov/st/texttrans-english/2009/February/20090219163832eaifas0.5075342.html; "China Puts Breaks on Talks with Japan, U.S.," *Japan Times*, July 31, 2009, http://search.japantimes.co.jp/cgi-bin/nn20090731a4.html; Cui Xiaohuo, "U.S.-Japan-China Talks to Focus on Key Issues," *China Daily*, June 8, 2009, http://www.chinadaily.com.cn/china/2009-06/08/content_8257370.htm.
9. Yoichi Funabashi, "Forget Bretton Woods II: The Role for U.S.-China-Japan Trilateralism," *Washington Quarterly*, April 2009, pp. 7–25.

10. Marc Grossman, "The Tsunami Core Group: A Step Toward a Transformed Diplomacy in Asia and Beyond," *Security Challenges* 1, no. 1 (2005), pp. 11–14.
11. American policymakers have promoted ad hoc approaches before, but with too little effect on the multilateral arrangements that have emerged in Asia. See, for instance, James A. Baker III, "America in Asia: Emerging Architecture for a Pacific Community," *Foreign Affairs*, Winter 1991/92, http://www.foreignaffairs.com/articles/47433/james-a-baker-iii/america-in-asia-emerging-architecture-for-a-pacific-community.
12. For an example of one such proposal, see James Goodby and Markku Heiskanen, "Old Ideas and New Diplomats: A Fresh Beginning in Northeast Asia?" Nautilus Institute Policy Forum Online 09-034A, April 29, 2009, http://www.nautilus.org/fora/security/09034GoodbyHeiskanen.html.
13. Robert B. Zoellick, "After the Crisis," remarks at the Paul H. Nitze School of Advanced International Studies, Johns Hopkins University, September 28, 2009, http://web.worldbank.org/WBSITE/EXTERNAL/NEWS/0,,contentMDK:22329125~pagePK:34370~piPK:42770~theSitePK:4607,00.html.
14. Hadi Soesastro, "Kevin Rudd's Architecture for the Asia Pacific," *East Asia Forum*, August 14, 2008, http://www.csis.or.id/scholars_opinion_view.asp?op_id=683&id=14&tab=0.
15. Jusuf Wanandi, "Remodeling Regional Architecture," *PacNet*, no. 13 (February 18, 2009), http://csis.org/files/media/csis/pubs/pac0913.pdf.
16. C. Fred Bergsten, "Pacific Asia and the Asia Pacific: The Choices for APEC," Policy Brief 09-16 (Washington, DC: Peterson Institute for International Economics, July 2009), pp. 3–4.
17. Barry Desker, "Why APEC Needs Results in Sydney," *RSIS Commentaries*, September 2007, http://www.rsis.edu.sg/publications/Perspective/RSIS0952007.pdf.
18. "Japan Shelves Military Aid Flight," *BBC News*, May 30, 2008, http://news.bbc.co.uk/2/hi/7426899.stm.
19. Senator Richard G. Lugar, "Lugar ASEAN Proposal Enacted by Administration," press release, August 10, 2006, http://lugar.senate.gov/press/record.cfm?id=261634; Singapore Ministry of Foreign Affairs, "Singapore Welcomes Confirmation of the United States Ambassador for ASEAN Affairs," press release, May 1, 2008, http://www.41amm.sg/amm/index.php/web/press_room/press_releases/singapore_welcomes_confirmation_of_the_united_states_ambassador_for_asean_affairs.
20. U.S. Agency for International Development, "The ASEAN-United States Enhanced Partnership," http://www.asean-us-partnership.org/index.htm.

About the Authors

Evan A. Feigenbaum is senior fellow for East, Central, and South Asia at the Council on Foreign Relations. From 2001 to 2009, he served at the U.S. Department of State in various capacities: as deputy assistant secretary of state for South Asia, deputy assistant secretary of state for Central Asia, member of the policy planning staff with principal responsibility for East Asia and the Pacific, and as an adviser on China to Deputy Secretary of State Robert B. Zoellick, with whom he worked closely in the development of the U.S.-China senior dialogue. During the intensive final phase of the U.S.-India civil nuclear initiative from July to October 2008, he co-chaired the coordinating team charged with moving the agreement through the International Atomic Energy Agency Board of Governors and the Nuclear Suppliers Group, and then to Congress, where it became the U.S.-India Nuclear Cooperation Approval and Nonproliferation Enhancement Act. He received the department's Superior Honor Award five times.

Before his government service, Dr. Feigenbaum worked at Harvard University, where he was lecturer on government in the Faculty of Arts and Sciences, and executive director of the Asia–Pacific Security Initiative and program chair of the Chinese security studies program in the John F. Kennedy School of Government. His books include *China's Techno-Warriors: National Security and Strategic Competition from the Nuclear to the Information Age*. He received his AB in history from the University of Michigan and his AM and PhD in political science from Stanford University.

Robert A. Manning is a senior adviser to the Atlantic Council. The views in this special report are solely his own and do not represent the U.S. government or any U.S. government agency. Mr. Manning served at the U.S. Department of State from 2001 to 2008, on the policy planning staff and as senior counselor for energy, technology, and science policy. As senior counselor, he advised the undersecretary of state for global affairs and other senior officials on a range of issues, including energy and climate change policy, new energy technologies, development and the Millennium Challenge Account, science and technology issues, and North Korea and Iran nuclear issues. He also was one of the creators of the Global Issues Forum with India and subsequently with China.

From 1997 to 2001, Mr. Manning was director of Asia studies and a senior fellow at the Council on Foreign Relations, where he led several Task Force studies, including Task Forces on Korea and Southeast Asia. From 1989 to 1993, Mr. Manning was an adviser for policy and public diplomacy to the assistant secretary of state for East Asian and Pacific affairs. Prior to this, he was an adviser to the office of the secretary of defense. His publications include *The Asian Energy Factor*; the CFR report *China, Nuclear Weapons, and Arms Control*; essays on nuclear weapons; numerous journal articles on international energy and Asian security issues; and book chapters in edited volumes on China, Korea, Japan, energy, and energy security.

Advisory Committee for *The United States in the New Asia*

Morton I. Abramowitz
The Century Foundation

Richard L. Armitage
Armitage International L.C.

Charlene Barshefsky
WilmerHale

Chas. W. Freeman Jr.
Projects International, Inc.

Ellen L. Frost
Peter G. Peterson Institute for International Economics and *National Defense University*

Michael J. Green
Center for Strategic & International Studies

James A. Kelly

Sukhan Kim
Akin, Gump, Strauss, Hauer & Feld LLP

Nicholas R. Lardy
Peter G. Peterson Institute for International Economics

Richard P. Lawless
Richard Lawless and Associates

Kevin G. Nealer
Forum for International Policy

Marcus Noland
Peter G. Peterson Institute for International Economics

Joseph S. Nye Jr.
Harvard University

Douglas H. Paal
Carnegie Endowment for International Peace

James J. Przystup
National Defense University

Mitchell B. Reiss
College of William & Mary

Stanley Owen Roth
The Boeing Company

J. Stapleton Roy
Woodrow Wilson International Center for Scholars

James J. Shinn
Princeton University

Note: Council Special Reports reflect the judgments and recommendations of the author(s). They do not necessarily represent the views of members of the advisory committee, whose involvement in no way should be interpreted as an endorsement of the report by either themselves or the organizations with which they are affiliated.

Mission Statement of the International Institutions and Global Governance Program

The International Institutions and Global Governance (IIGG) program at CFR aims to identify the institutional requirements for effective multilateral cooperation in the twenty-first century. The program is motivated by recognition that the architecture of global governance—largely reflecting the world as it existed in 1945—has not kept pace with fundamental changes in the international system. These shifts include the spread of transnational challenges, the rise of new powers, and the mounting influence of nonstate actors. Existing multilateral arrangements thus provide an inadequate foundation for addressing many of today's most pressing threats and opportunities and for advancing U.S. national and broader global interests.

Given these trends, U.S. policymakers and other interested actors require rigorous, independent analysis of current structures of multilateral cooperation, and of the promises and pitfalls of alternative institutional arrangements. The IIGG program meets these needs by analyzing the strengths and weaknesses of existing multilateral institutions and proposing reforms tailored to new international circumstances.

The IIGG program fulfills its mandate by

- Engaging CFR fellows in research on improving existing and building new frameworks to address specific global challenges—including climate change, the proliferation of weapons of mass destruction, transnational terrorism, and global health—and disseminating the research through books, articles, Council Special Reports, and other outlets;
- Bringing together influential foreign policymakers, scholars, and CFR members to debate the merits of international regimes and frameworks at meetings in New York, Washington, DC, and other select cities;

- Hosting roundtable series whose objectives are to inform the foreign policy community of today's international governance challenges and breed inventive solutions to strengthen the world's multilateral bodies; and
- Providing a state-of-the-art Web presence as a resource to the wider foreign policy community on issues related to the future of global governance.

Council Special Reports

Published by the Council on Foreign Relations

Intervention to Stop Genocide and Mass Atrocities: International Norms and U.S. Policy
Matthew C. Waxman; CSR No. 49, October 2009
An International Institutions and Global Governance Program Report

Enhancing U.S. Preventive Action
Paul B. Stares and Micah Zenko; CSR No. 48, October 2009
A Center for Preventive Action Report

The Canadian Oil Sands: Energy Security vs. Climate Change
Michael A. Levi; CSR No. 47, May 2009
A Maurice R. Greenberg Center for Geoeconomic Studies Report

The National Interest and the Law of the Sea
Scott G. Borgerson; CSR No. 46, May 2009

Lessons of the Financial Crisis
Benn Steil; CSR No. 45, March 2009
A Maurice R. Greenberg Center for Geoeconomic Studies Report

Global Imbalances and the Financial Crisis
Steven Dunaway; CSR No. 44, March 2009
A Maurice R. Greenberg Center for Geoeconomic Studies Report

Eurasian Energy Security
Jeffrey Mankoff; CSR No. 43, February 2009

Preparing for Sudden Change in North Korea
Paul B. Stares and Joel S. Wit; CSR No. 42, January 2009
A Center for Preventive Action Report

Averting Crisis in Ukraine
Steven Pifer; CSR No. 41, January 2009
A Center for Preventive Action Report

Congo: Securing Peace, Sustaining Progress
Anthony W. Gambino; CSR No. 40, October 2008
A Center for Preventive Action Report

Deterring State Sponsorship of Nuclear Terrorism
Michael A. Levi; CSR No. 39, September 2008

China, Space Weapons, and U.S. Security
Bruce W. MacDonald; CSR No. 38, September 2008

Sovereign Wealth and Sovereign Power: The Strategic Consequences of American Indebtedness
Brad W. Setser; CSR No. 37, September 2008
A Maurice R. Greenberg Center for Geoeconomic Studies Report

Securing Pakistan's Tribal Belt
Daniel Markey; CSR No. 36, July 2008 (Web-only release) and August 2008
A Center for Preventive Action Report

Avoiding Transfers to Torture
Ashley S. Deeks; CSR No. 35, June 2008

Global FDI Policy: Correcting a Protectionist Drift
David M. Marchick and Matthew J. Slaughter; CSR No. 34, June 2008
A Maurice R. Greenberg Center for Geoeconomic Studies Report

Dealing with Damascus: Seeking a Greater Return on U.S.-Syria Relations
Mona Yacoubian and Scott Lasensky; CSR No. 33, June 2008
A Center for Preventive Action Report

Climate Change and National Security: An Agenda for Action
Joshua W. Busby; CSR No. 32, November 2007
A Maurice R. Greenberg Center for Geoeconomic Studies Report

Planning for Post-Mugabe Zimbabwe
Michelle D. Gavin; CSR No. 31, October 2007
A Center for Preventive Action Report

The Case for Wage Insurance
Robert J. LaLonde; CSR No. 30, September 2007
A Maurice R. Greenberg Center for Geoeconomic Studies Report

Reform of the International Monetary Fund
Peter B. Kenen; CSR No. 29, May 2007
A Maurice R. Greenberg Center for Geoeconomic Studies Report

Nuclear Energy: Balancing Benefits and Risks
Charles D. Ferguson; CSR No. 28, April 2007

Nigeria: Elections and Continuing Challenges
Robert I. Rotberg; CSR No. 27, April 2007
A Center for Preventive Action Report

The Economic Logic of Illegal Immigration
Gordon H. Hanson; CSR No. 26, April 2007
A Maurice R. Greenberg Center for Geoeconomic Studies Report

The United States and the WTO Dispute Settlement System
Robert Z. Lawrence; CSR No. 25, March 2007
A Maurice R. Greenberg Center for Geoeconomic Studies Report

Bolivia on the Brink
Eduardo A. Gamarra; CSR No. 24, February 2007
A Center for Preventive Action Report

After the Surge: The Case for U.S. Military Disengagement from Iraq
Steven N. Simon; CSR No. 23, February 2007

Darfur and Beyond: What Is Needed to Prevent Mass Atrocities
Lee Feinstein; CSR No. 22, January 2007

Avoiding Conflict in the Horn of Africa: U.S. Policy Toward Ethiopia and Eritrea
Terrence Lyons; CSR No. 21, December 2006
A Center for Preventive Action Report

Living with Hugo: U.S. Policy Toward Hugo Chávez's Venezuela
Richard Lapper; CSR No. 20, November 2006
A Center for Preventive Action Report

Reforming U.S. Patent Policy: Getting the Incentives Right
Keith E. Maskus; CSR No. 19, November 2006
A Maurice R. Greenberg Center for Geoeconomic Studies Report

Foreign Investment and National Security: Getting the Balance Right
Alan P. Larson and David M. Marchick; CSR No. 18, July 2006
A Maurice R. Greenberg Center for Geoeconomic Studies Report

Challenges for a Postelection Mexico: Issues for U.S. Policy
Pamela K. Starr; CSR No. 17, June 2006 (Web-only release) and November 2006

U.S.-India Nuclear Cooperation: A Strategy for Moving Forward
Michael A. Levi and Charles D. Ferguson; CSR No. 16, June 2006

Generating Momentum for a New Era in U.S.-Turkey Relations
Steven A. Cook and Elizabeth Sherwood-Randall; CSR No. 15, June 2006

Peace in Papua: Widening a Window of Opportunity
Blair A. King; CSR No. 14, March 2006
A Center for Preventive Action Report

Neglected Defense: Mobilizing the Private Sector to Support Homeland Security
Stephen E. Flynn and Daniel B. Prieto; CSR No. 13, March 2006

Afghanistan's Uncertain Transition From Turmoil to Normalcy
Barnett R. Rubin; CSR No. 12, March 2006
A Center for Preventive Action Report

Preventing Catastrophic Nuclear Terrorism
Charles D. Ferguson; CSR No. 11, March 2006

Getting Serious About the Twin Deficits
Menzie D. Chinn; CSR No. 10, September 2005
A Maurice R. Greenberg Center for Geoeconomic Studies Report

Both Sides of the Aisle: A Call for Bipartisan Foreign Policy
Nancy E. Roman; CSR No. 9, September 2005

Forgotten Intervention? What the United States Needs to Do in the Western Balkans
Amelia Branczik and William L. Nash; CSR No. 8, June 2005
A Center for Preventive Action Report

A New Beginning: Strategies for a More Fruitful Dialogue with the Muslim World
Craig Charney and Nicole Yakatan; CSR No. 7, May 2005

Power-Sharing in Iraq
David L. Phillips; CSR No. 6, April 2005
A Center for Preventive Action Report

Giving Meaning to "Never Again": Seeking an Effective Response to the Crisis in Darfur and Beyond
Cheryl O. Igiri and Princeton N. Lyman; CSR No. 5, September 2004

Freedom, Prosperity, and Security: The G8 Partnership with Africa: Sea Island 2004 and Beyond
J. Brian Atwood, Robert S. Browne, and Princeton N. Lyman; CSR No. 4, May 2004

Addressing the HIV/AIDS Pandemic: A U.S. Global AIDS Strategy for the Long Term
Daniel M. Fox and Princeton N. Lyman; CSR No. 3, May 2004
Cosponsored with the Milbank Memorial Fund

Challenges for a Post-Election Philippines
Catharin E. Dalpino; CSR No. 2, May 2004
A Center for Preventive Action Report

Stability, Security, and Sovereignty in the Republic of Georgia
David L. Phillips; CSR No. 1, January 2004
A Center for Preventive Action Report

To purchase a printed copy, call the Brookings Institution Press: 800.537.5487.
Note: Council Special Reports are available for download from CFR's website, www.cfr.org.
For more information, email publications@cfr.org.